MINDFULNESS WORKBOOK FOR ANXIETY

MINDFULNESS WORKBOOK FOR ANXIETY

A Guide To Stress Relief and Anxiety Reduction With The Help of Daily Meditation

RACHEL STONE

Rachel Stone

Mindfulness Workbook For Anxiety:

A Guide To Stress Relief and Anxiety Reduction With The Help of Daily Meditation

by

Rachel Stone

intended only for informational purposes and should thus be thought of as universal. As befitting its nature, it is presented without assurance regarding its prolonged validity or interim quality. Trademarks that are mentioned are done without written consent and can in no way be considered an endorsement from the trademark holder.

Table of Contents

TABLE OF CONTENTS

INTRODUCTION

CHAPTER 1: WHAT IS MINDFULNESS?

CHAPTER 2: THE MODEL THE BOOK USES

CHAPTER 3: FINDING YOUR TRIGGERS

CHAPTER 4: BEGINNING YOUR MINDFULNESS PRACTICE

CHAPTER 5: ANXIETY MINDFULNESS MEDITATION

CHAPTER 6: SOCIAL ANXIETY MINDFULNESS MEDITATION

CHAPTER 7: TEST ANXIETY MINDFULNESS MEDITATION

CHAPTER 8: OCD MINDFULNESS MEDITATION

CHAPTER 9: TRAUMA RECOVERY MINDFULNESS MEDITATION

CONCLUSION

ADDITIONAL RESOURCES

MY OTHER BOOKS

ABOUT THE AUTHOR

1

What Is Mindfulness?

This book is all about using the power of your thoughts to be mindful and bring peace, purpose, and happiness to your life.

Mindfulness meditation is all about using your thoughts to be present in the moment and crafting the world that you want to live in. If you want to use mindfulness to help with your anxiety, this book is for you. Mindfulness mediation has been shown to have extraordinary effects on your life from your mental to physical health. This book will show you how to tap into the beautiful power of mindfulness meditation no matter if you are Buddhist or not.

Mindfulness Workbook For Anxiety: A Guide To Stress Relief and Anxiety Reduction With The Help of Daily Meditation covers nine chapters. In chapter 1, an overview of mindfulness meditation will be given. The subject of chapter 2 is about the mindfulness model the book uses to help improve your anxiety. Practical tips about identifying your anxiety-inducing triggers will be given in Chapter 3. How to start your mindfulness meditation practice will be explored in Chapter 4. Chapters 5-9 will give you mindfulness meditation scripts, writing prompts and exercises to help you deal with various anxieties such as day-to-day anxiety, social, test, OCD and trauma recovery meditation. The scripts included will help you get started so you do not have to start your meditation practice from scratch.

As you read, feel free to bookmark and highlight any passages that may be helpful so you can revisit these sections later. You can even take a pen and paper, and take notes the old-school way. With an easy-to-understand reading style and an informative and conversational tone, *Mindfulness Workbook For Anxiety: A Guide To Stress Relief and Anxiety Reduction With The Help of Daily Meditation* will more than prepare you to begin your journey into mindfulness and meditation. There are a lot of famous people who practice mindfulness like Naomie Harris, Boris Johnson, Katy Perry, Richard Branson, and Anderson Cooper to name a few; thus, you are in great company.

There are plenty of books on this subject on the market, thanks again for choosing this one! Every effort was made to ensure it is full of as much useful information as possible, please enjoy!

How many times have we been encouraged to see the cup half full instead of half-empty? Oftentimes in western society, the push to be optimistic and to think positive is drilled into us from a young age. However, if one is beginning to become more mindful, the transition to mindfulness may feel a little jarring, as it is opposite of what feels comfortable. Imagine this. Instead of focusing just on the positive aspect of life, mindfulness encourages a realistic outlook on life that embraces the good and the bad, the positive, the negative and the neutral. And this is where our book begins, starting off by learning about this effective way of living that has been used successfully for centuries – mindfulness meditation.

Buddhist monks have been using the power of mindfulness for over 2,500 years. Mindfulness is the act of allowing your brain to rest while observing the thoughts that come and go in your mind. Mindfulness meditation is different from actively thinking and using your creative mind. When you are being mindful, you focus on an object, scene or sound that is calm and then let your thoughts gently amble by in your mind. Being mindful is powerful because if you are always caught up into being busy and always thinking about your next step, mindfulness gives you a much-needed break and makes you reflect on your pattern of thoughts and actions. It is the exact opposite of the daily living experience of most people because instead of going, mindfulness encourages you to slow down the pace.

Mindfulness allows you to know your thoughts instead of trying to change them. Instead of being judgmental and unkind to yourself if you think something negative, mindfulness has no judgement value on your thoughts. Your thoughts are just there. When you are mindful, you are taking notes of your thoughts like a note-taker. When you are in a mindful state, you just pay attention to what your thoughts are doing but giving them the freedom to do what they want. Ultimately, the goal of mindfulness is to know your mind. Once you begin to know your mind, you can begin the next step which is to train your mind to help you deal with your anxiety.

The beautiful thing about our minds is that they are malleable, and as a result, they are trainable. Our minds are able to change based on what one is thinking. If you think the world is a horrible place, you will operate from a place of fear and your actions will show that. If you think that the world is a wonderful place, you will operate from a place of reckless optimism without being able to be realistic about certain dangers you may find yourself in. Mindfulness helps you to know your thoughts and then begin to train your thoughts to help deal with your anxiety. Mindfulness slows down the grind of your busy daily pace and gives you a different vantage point about patterns in in your life. These patterns can be feelings that you have in certain situations or your reactions to how other people treat you. When you are being mindful, you may notice trends and patterns that you are constantly thinking. Are you always wanting more and more? Do you feel comfortable with the way things are? Whatever patterns you notice, mindfulness can help you pinpoint what types of things are causing you mental anguish, conflict, or joy. Then after noticing these patterns, you can begin to shape it to how you would like to be by focusing on being more gracious, compassionate, and kind with your thoughts.

When you begin your practice, do not treat your mindfulness meditation practices as an obligatory item on your daily to-do list. The most important thing to remember before you begin is that you are training your mind to be at peace with how things are going in the world, no matter what is happening. Once you are able to be at peace in no matter what situation you find yourself in, then you are able to start to work on yourself to change your reactions to your anxiety. Mindfulness meditation is not a sprint; it is a marathon that you continually work on until you are finally able to free yourself from unsavory anxiety-filled emotions.

When you are training your mind to be more mindful, affirmations are great tools to use. Affirmations are very helpful, especially when you create them yourself. The thought process behind using affirmations is to use very direct language which influences your subconscious to help you get the outcome that you want to get. When you use affirmations, you want to first figure out what outcome it is that you want. Then create a short sentence with an active word. Make sure the sentence is in the present tense. For example, if you want to feel calmer and not be so anxiety-ridden, you can create an affirmation to help. You will start with the outcome of being calmer and make that into a statement using the present tense. Thus, the affirmation would be 'I am more calm.' By using the present tense, you are affirming the future outcome. When the affirmation is created, you can say it during your meditation time and throughout the day. When you couple this practice of saying affirmations with your mindfulness mediation session, they work doubly together to help you get the outcome that you want to get. For example, you hear the term think positive all the time. It is because positive thinking can help shape your future to where you have a positive future. However, if you think negative oftentimes a reality reflects your thoughts. Our thoughts influence our subconscious which in turn can determine our reality.

Mindfulness meditation helps you shape your reality by taking the time to know your mind. Once you know your mind, you will be able to train it and ultimately free it from negative, debilitating thinking. Every step works together. Before you begin your mindfulness meditation practice, know that it is not going to be easy. It will be a journey, but if you are dedicated, you will see a difference in your life.

Mindfulness is awesome because it:

- Helps you not be judgmental – One of the major components of mindfulness is to not be judgmental of yourself and others. This gentleness towards yourself improves your overall self-esteem, especially when suffering from anxiety. It also encourages self-compassion for yourself and for others.
- Easy and fast – There is no set time to do it. It is super easy to pick up on and relatively fast to do. Your sessions can be as long as they need to be or as short as they can be. If you have a busy schedule, you can meditate for 5 minutes or however long is best for you.
- Reduces stress instantly -Because the necessity of breathing is at the core of mindfulness meditation, deep breathing immediately reduces the stress you may feel as soon as you begin your mindfulness meditation session.

- Improves your wisdom – Mindfulness meditation improves your wisdom because you are able to figure out what makes you tick by noting and understanding the power of your thoughts. You also are able to be wise about other people, because this system meditation improves your observation skills such that you will be able to observe others and make connections about their behavior in ways that you have not been able to before.
- No set way to do it – For some people, the fact there is no set structure may be limited to them, but it is a positive because there is not a right or wrong way to do it.
- Relaxing and calms your nerves – Just like reducing your stress instantly, mindfulness meditation also relaxes and calms your nerves due to the power of breathing.
- Observe yourself in the moment – Mindfulness meditation allows you to be in tune with your thoughts and actions so you are able to get into the 'zone' a lot easier than before.
- Easy to pick-up – Did I mention how easy mindfulness meditation is to pick up? Once you have one session, you will be able to do more rather easily.
- Doesn't have to depend on anyone else to do it – Mindfulness meditation is great to practice on your own. So you never have to worry about if the teacher is going to show up to class or not. This meditation style is self-guided so you can set your schedule according to your convenience.

There are also tons of researched and proven health benefits of doing mindfulness meditation. Mindfulness meditation is a factor in:

- Managing pain that's chronic – Mindfulness helps you strengthen your focus so you are able to focus on other things so that you can manage your pain.
- Reducing anxiety, stress, and depression -Again, the breath and it is healing power makes mindfulness meditation phenomenal at relieving issues with stress, depression, and anxiety. People who practice mindfulness meditation regularly oftentimes have lower blood pressure and a stronger immune system.
- Helps you sleep better -The relaxation that comes from mindfulness meditation helps you home in on the triggers that help you sleep. It is a surefire sleep aid.
- Helps elderly and pregnant women – Mindfulness meditation does a great job of helping elderly people not feel so alone, anyone for that matter, and it is also a great labor tool for pregnant women.
- Improves intuition and creativity – Mindfulness meditation is a favorite of creatives and helps improve the creativity in non-creatives, too.

As you can see, mindfulness is an effective way to help deal with your anxiety. The next chapter will go into more detail about mindfulness meditation practices that will help you deal with your anxiety.

2

The Model The Book Uses

Mindfulness Workbook For Anxiety: A Guide To Stress Relief and Anxiety Reduction With The Help of Daily Meditation draws from the Mindfulness-Based Stress Reduction group program or MBSR. Jon Kabat-Zinn developed this program in the 1970s to help patients who are struggling with life's difficulties such as anxiety, mental or physical illness. Even though initially created to help hospital patients, it has been used to help a lot of people throughout life. The beauty of the MBSR is that it is customized to the individual's needs instead of following strict rules. The most important aspect of MBSR is to be consistent. We ask that you set aside an amount of time daily to do the work in order to help with your anxiety. Using this approach will help you become more aware of the connection between your mind and body in an effort to move your limiting beliefs, behaviors, and feelings that are at the core of your anxiety.

With each mindfulness exercise, there will be a guided meditation script, writing prompts that will help you explore your anxiety and cope with it. Each exercise is about 5-15 minutes and can be done no matter how busy your schedule may be. You will have space to work through your thoughts, reflect, cope and adjust. They are perfect for helping you to slip into meditation practice no matter if you have a yoga background or not or if this is your first time meditating.

The rest of this chapter will give you core mindfulness and breathing trainings that will form the basis of the exercises later in the book. To begin, we will focus on different breathing exercises. The first technique is called left and right nostril breathing. This technique is interesting because, at any time, we inhale and exhale though one nostril more times than the other nostril. This pattern changes every 90 to 150 minutes. Our nostrils are connected to opposite sides of our brains. So our left nostril is connected to our right nostril and the right nostril is connected to the left side of the brain. This technique is great breathing exercise, but it also helps you deal with qualities associated with the particular nostril. For example, the left nostril connects to the right side of the brain is associated with sensitivity, synthesis, calmness, empathy, receptive and cleansing energy. The right nostril connects to the left side of the brain and is associated with concentration, vim, will power, gumption, alertness, warmth and nurturing energy. To do the exercise, you want to put your right thumb over your right nostril and then inhale solely through your left nostril. Then take your ring finger and put it over the left nostril so you can exhale out of the right nostril. Then keep your fingers there to inhale in your right nostril, then switch fingers and cover the right nostril so you can exhale out your left nostril. Then repeat on each site. This exercise can be tricky so be careful to take note of which nostril you are inhaling and exhaling out of to prevent confusion. This exercise is great for helping you to gain clarity and sharpen your discipline skills.

Equal breathing is another important foundational breathing exercise to know. We've already covered it somewhat but did not mention the specific name. For equal breathing, you get comfortable and then inhale through your nose for 3 counts and then exhale from your nose for a minimum of 3 counts. The important part of equal breathing is to remember to inhale the same number of counts on every inhale and inhale. You can do more than 3 counts of breathing, just make sure that you do the same count on each side. Abdominal breathing, or diaphragmatic breathing is at the crux of your breathing exercises. It is also called deep breathing, and it is simply a deep breath that draws from your diaphragm rather than your chest. If it feels weird to breathe from your diaphragm, you should practice diaphragmatic breathing. This method helps your inhales get deeper. You can also put one hand on your chest and another hand on your ribcage to make your breathing deeper. Doing this allows you to feel your breath going in and going out. This breathing technique also helps prevent you from breathing through your chest only. By breathing through your diaphragm improves your lung and digestive functions, too.

The next awesome breathing exercise is called 4-7-8 breathing. For the 4-7-8 breathing exercise, you get comfortable. Then begin by exhaling through your mouth and try to make a 'whoosh' sound. Next, you will need to begin to inhale through your mouth. Close your mouth from the previous exhale and when you inhale, hold the inhaled breath for at least to the count of four which you will count in your mind. Next, hold your breath for 7 seconds. If you are initially unable to start at 7 seconds, that's ok. Hold your breath for as long as possible. Then exhale again, but this time make the 'whoosh' sound to the count of eight in your mind. You can make the breath slow and steady so it can last to the full eight counts. The entire sequence is considered one breath. It is best to start slow with this exercise then increase the speed. When you begin, try to keep the 4-7-8 count as close as possible so you can nail the correct breathing technique.

Since we've discussed breathing exercises, now it is time to begin discussing relaxation exercises. Relaxation is important because it helps heal your anxiety and stress. It improves your skin and your heartbeat and breathing which in turn improves your overall reaction to chronic stress. Without proper rest and relaxation, your body begins to break down because you have no way to rejuvenate yourself. While you may be good at the breathing exercises, your brain may still have racing thoughts. By coupling the relaxation methods with your breathing exercises, you are able to add another layer of stillness to your meditation practice which will make you more aware and present at the moment.

The first relaxation exercise is called autogenic relaxation. The concept behind autogenic relaxation is that you have everything your body needs to relax. (Autogenic means self-regulation or self-generated.) With this method, you visualize that your body is warm and relaxed. The autogenic relaxation method is great for stabilizing your heartbeat, relaxing your entire body and helping you achieve deep breathing. The method is easy. You first begin by finding a nice comfortable place to relax. Then you mentally work your way through visualizing warmth or calmness coming to every part of your body. The warm and calm feeling helps you feel relaxed like you are in a cozy blanket. Begin from the top of your body and work your way down or begin at the bottom of your body and work your way up.

For example, when doing at autogenic exercise (going from the top of your body to the bottom of your body), you begin by feeling relaxed in your head. You can imagine that your head is experiencing a wonderful burst of calm and loving warmth. Then imagine that the feeling of warmth has made its way to your forehead area. You can feel the warmth cause your forehead to tingle and melt all your tension away. Next, you'll want to follow the warm feeling all the way down to your stomach area. Repeat to yourself that your stomach is warm. Then feel the warmth travel down your legs, thighs, shins, and toes, warming every part until you get to the bottom of your feet.

While doing this type of exercise, you can also turn your attention to your breathing at any time. Note how calm and energy-giving your breaths are. You can also focus on your heartbeat and note how steady your heartbeat. It is also great to feel how your heartbeat sends warmth and relaxation throughout the rest of your body, especially your extremities like your arms and legs. Other phrases (or variations thereof) you can say while doing an autogenic meditation are that 'I feel relaxed.' or 'My body feels calm and quiet and comfortable.' or even 'I feel the warmth radiating throughout my body which relaxes and calms me.' (These are a few phrases that can help you get started.) Once you finish, imagine yourself doing an activity that you love. Whether that is relaxing on the beach or playing on the playground with your inner child. The ending activity can even draw on a dear memory that made you feel loved, safe or confident. The ending thought is a comfortable way to transition from the total feeling of relaxation of the autogenic exercise back to your day-to-day life.

The visualization technique is the next form of mental exercise that you can use to relax. This exercise is also fun to do because it requires that you use your imagination. Do you remember when you were a kid and you always used your imagination? It seems like the use of imagination gets lost the older we become. However, with this visualization exercise, you're able to tap into your imagination part of your brain and go back to using your imagination like in your childhood days. A visualization meditation session is similar to daydreaming in that you think of images that may you feel happy. However, visualization is active and present in helping you figure out how to relax your body by using your senses to think of imagery that helps you relax. Normally, daydreaming usually takes into account memories that make you feel good, whereas, a visualization exercise would observe a negative memory, make note of it, and then return back to the more pleasant feeling. A visualization exercise is also different from a guided meditation because you are in charge of finding the memories of what you're most comfortable with instead of relying on the guided meditation to help you visualize images that help you relax. Lastly, and distinctly, a visualization meditation exercise draws upon all of your senses of touch, taste, seeing, hearing and smelling to visualize the most relaxing moments to so that you can experience a state of relaxation for your entire body.

To begin a visualization exercise, you first must find a comfortable position in your special place. Once you are comfortable, think of an image that makes you feel warm and relaxed. This image can be of you walking on the beach. You can imagine the warm wind whipping at your hair or the warm sun extending its warmth over your body. You can smell the fresh scent of the ocean spray and accidentally taste the salty spray of the ocean as you dip into a way. You can hear seagulls loudly cawing in the turquoise blue sky while the gritty sand can be between your toes. While you are visualizing, do not forget to breathe deeply. You can inhale through your nose and exhale through your mouth. After you finish one visual image, you can transition into a different one. Do not feel like you have to stick to one visualization throughout your meditation session. You can transition back and forth between different imagery.

For example, after visualizing a peaceful beach scene, you can transition to a visual image of you sitting at a holiday dinner table surrounded by family members and friends that you love. The scents of your favorite foods fill the air. Foods like freshly baked bread, cheesy macaroni and cheese, roasted chicken and your favorite desserts fill the air. You can even smell the scents of your favorite person, whether its leathery, fruity or more flowery. What other scents do you smell? After you work through one sense, like the smell, you'll work through all the rest of the senses. How does the food taste when you eat it? Do your taste buds explode from goodness? Does the air taste warm from the heat in the kitchen? How does your clothing feel against you? Are you wearing your favorite blouse or shirt? Are you wearing jeans or some other type of material? Visualize the tight embrace from your grandma or parents. And what about the sounds? How loud is your aunt and uncle's laughter? Imagine the gentle cry of a newborn recently born into the family. How about the holiday playlist playing your favorite songs? Or imagine the lacy detail of the holiday tablecloth. What does the overall scene look like? Who are you sitting next to the table? If you do not sit at a table, how is the seating arranged? You can be as detailed as you would like as you go through the scene in order to get as many great memories during your visualization session. You can also go as fast as you would like or as slow as you like. Choose to end the visualization on a very happy memory and feel how relaxes your body is. Then take a deep breath and open your eyes so you can go about your day. This exercise is very helpful in helping you relax, and it is one of my favorite relaxation methods to use. You can also couple a visualization meditation session with the use of affirmations, especially if you already have a list of affirmations written. For example, after each image you visualize, you can say to yourself, 'I am relaxed.'; 'I am calm.' or 'I am happy.' after seeing it. You can also use your affirmations to visualize an outcome that you would like. If you are trying to reach a goal, you can visualize what it looks like when you reach the goal. Use all your senses to imagine the scene and use your affirmations after each scene as well.

For example, if you have a goal of receiving a promotion, you can do a visualization session of you receiving the promotion. Imagine how your boss' office will look like when you get the promotion. How does the office smell? What are you going to smell like? Will you have your favorite scent on? What will you eat for breakfast that day? Will your palms be sweaty? What will your celebration party look like? How will your friends, family, and coworkers act? After each image, say an affirmation, like, 'I work hard, and I am worthy of a promotion.' 'I can do anything I put my mind to.' to name a few. Remember, the more detailed you are, the more helpful the session is. This is a powerful tool to have in your meditation arsenal.

The last relaxation technique examined in this chapter is called progressive relaxation. Progressive relaxation is also known as body scan meditation. The technique behind progressive relaxation is to relieve your anxiety levels, too. This method of relaxation is powerful because when your body is physically relaxed you cannot be anxious. If you are experiencing an anxiety attack or feeling anxious, by the end of a progressive relaxation session, your anxiety should be gone, and your body should be completely relaxed. If you have chronic anxiety, this tool helps you relieve the anxiety outside of using medication. This method is also great at helping relieve chronic pain because it helps you relax and take the focus off the pain. Progressive relaxation involves a simple two-step process. First you tense the muscle group that you are working on and then you let the tension out by relaxing the muscles. You will then take notice of how the relaxed state feels which helps you relax easier the more you do this method. You can either begin at the bottom of your body and then you work up or you can begin at the top of your body and work your way down. Before you start, make sure that you are in a comfortable position lying down on your back. Then you can begin.

- With your first muscle group or body part, breathe in, and tense the first muscle group (Tense firmly, but not to the point of pain or cramping.) for about 4 to 10 seconds. Be mindful that you do not tense too hard and cause pain which defeats the purpose of the exercise
- Then breathe out and completely relax the muscle group as quickly as you can (do not relax it gradually).
- Keep the muscle group or body part in the relaxed state for about 10 to 20 seconds before you work on the next muscle group.
- Notice the difference between how the muscles feel when they are tense and how they feel when they are relaxed. The relaxed state is helpful to know so if you ever needed to relax without doing this body scan, your muscle memory can kick in.
- When you are finished with all of the muscle groups, count backward from 5 to 1 to bring your focus back to the present.

The great thing about this technique is you do not have to be tense in order to practice it. It is best to practice it when you are calm so when you are anxious you are able to go through the steps without being confused since you've already practiced it. The body map you can follow when doing the body scan can look like this. You can start on one side and do one side completely and then go to the other side of your body. You can also do both sides at the same time before progressing to the next side of your body. This example body scan goes from the bottom of your body to the top of your body, by doing one side at a time.

3

Finding Your Triggers

- Feet - Wiggle your toes and point them to your face. Then point your toes downward. If you feel any tension from the waist down when you do this, relax your body.
- Lower foot and leg - Make your calf muscles tense by pointing your toes towards you.
- Thighs - Squeeze them hard and then let them go.
- Entire leg -Squeeze your thighs again and note any tension you may experience. Release the tension.
- Glutes - Squeeze your butt together and then release them.
- Hips - Roll your hips around and then let them go.
- Stomach - Hold your stomach in and then let it go.
- Back - Arch your stomach away from where you are resting and then bring it back down.

- Chest - Take a very deep breath for 5 to 15 seconds.
- Hand - Close your fist as tightly as possible and then let it go.
- Upper arms and biceps - Squeeze your fingers into a fist, bend your arm at your elbow and then flex your bicep in the muscle formation.
- Forearms and wrists - Extend them and bend your hands back at your wrist.
- Shoulders - Perform a shrug. Try to bring your shoulders at high as possible, aim for your ear, and let the shrug go.
- Front of the neck - Move your chin downward and try not to cause tension in your head and neck when you do it.
- Back of the neck - Press your head into the floor as far back as possible.
- Your mouth and the area around your mouth - Purse your lips as tightly as possible.
- Jaws and cheeks - Smile the widest smile that you can.
- Around the bridge of your nose and eyes - Wiggle your nose and then close your eyes as tightly as possible.
- Forehead - Frown as deeply as possible and wrinkle your forehead while you do so.

Once you finish going to the top on one side and make it to your forehead, you can go back down throughout the rest of your body. Once you are great at practicing the entire body, you can make the exercise shorter by doing a shorter version that focuses on the main body parts. You can also pick and choose what body parts you would like to scan so you can create your own customized progressive scan. A shortened body scan example would look like this:

- Lower limbs (legs and feet) – Point your toes upward, tense your calves and squeeze your thighs on both sides.
- Stomach and chest – Breathe in and breathe out as deeply as possible and feel your stomach contract as far as possible.
- Shoulders, arms, neck – Raise your shoulders up high as possible and let them go. You can flex your biceps and then bend your wrists as far back as possible. Be sure to do this on both sides of your body.
- Face – Wrinkle your forehead and the area around your nose. Smile as widely as possible and frown as widely as possible to work your entire face.

After becoming a pro at knowing how your body feels when it is relaxed. You can then focus on the relaxed or released part only. You can do the full body by relaxing or the shortened body. Initially, the release only technique may feel different as it will feel less intense that the full tense and release exercise, but the more you practice, the more you feel comfortable with the full exercise. Practicing these breathing exercises and relaxation techniques whether you are stressed or not is a great way to help deal with your anxiety. When you know how your body reacts to these techniques and how your body feels when you do them will only help you be that much more effective when you are fighting your anxiety.

Great job working through this chapter! Hopefully, you've made plenty of notes and highlighted the exercises you want to try. This chapter highlighted all the ways that you can use breathing and relaxation exercises to add to your mindfulness meditation practice. Some breathing exercises also include popular breathing techniques such as equal breathing, 4-7-8 breathing, and left and right nostril breathing. Popular relaxation methods covered in the chapter are autogenic relaxation, progressive relaxation, and visualization techniques. The next two chapters will focus on helping you identify and begin noting what triggers your anxiety so you can find a way to manage your anxiety better.

Mindfulness meditation is all about being present in every moment of your life. Consistent mindfulness meditation helps you to be energized, loving, caring, forgiving and compassionate regardless of the anxiety you may feel. You may not ever be able to get rid of anxiety, but you are able to identify triggers that may cause you anxiety and learn how to manage those triggers. This chapter will first highlight situations in which you may find yourself being anxious, identify the type of anxiety you may be feeling, and end with tips that can help you manage your anxiety.

There are many situations in which you may find your anxiety being triggered. These situations are numerous.

- Social anxiety can even anxious feelings towards those you have to deal with in everyday life. Common situations include social anxiety for when you have to deal with new or unfamiliar people. Some people even feel anxiety when dealing with people in their daily life.
- Test anxiety is the anxiety you can feel before major exams or tests. This type of anxiety isn't just limited

to students, but people who are waiting for medical results or any major test results can also suffer from this anxiety.

- Daily anxiety can occur from the day-to-day challenges such as managing households, people, finances, and responsibilities in life. This type of anxiety can be a cause of constant worry and an overwhelming feeling that makes you give up and not want to deal with life at all.

- OCD is an anxiety that comes from an incessant need to be in control at all times. This is the root cause of many larger forms of anxiety. If you can get this type of anxiety under control, you will notice an immediate difference in your life.

- Trauma recovery anxiety can be a result of dealing with trauma related concerns. Just because you make it through a trauma doesn't mean that the feelings associated with that trauma goes away. One must constantly explore and work through the feelings associated with the trauma.

If you are not sure what's causing y our anxiety, it may be time to explore the circumstances in your life more. Here are a few common causes of triggers that can cause anxiety. Our anxiety can stem from many situations that are unique to our daily living experience. This list is not comprehensive, but a great place to start.

Caffeine – Do you consume a lot of caffeine? Caffeine may taste great, but it does have anxiety-inducing properties. Try to switch to a non-caffeinated version of your favorite drink to see if that helps. Similarly, skipping meals can also contribute to anxiety so make sure that you are eating well-balanced meals at a reasonable time to prevent anxiety attacks caused by not eating healthy.

Your Medication – Are you taking any medications every day? Medications can contribute to your anxiety. Ask your doctor if there are different medications you can taste that help alleviates your anxiety or if you can give up certain medications altogether. In the same vein, if you are struggling with chronic illnesses, that may contribute to your anxiety. Speak with your preferred healthcare professional about ways to see if you can find a support group to deal with your health concerns.

Your Daily Schedule – Are you practicing great-time management skills? Having a jam-packed schedule can contribute to anxiety and make your days more stressful. If you are not using your time wisely, see if you can create a better schedule suited to your daily needs in an attempt to help with your stress.

Financial Concerns – Money issues can cause anxiety. Think of ways to address your financial needs instead of ignoring them. The peace of mind with coming up with a plan can do wonders for your anxiety.

Party Functions – Sometimes parties and other social gatherings can cause anxiety. See if you can take a friend or limit your interactions or improve your social awareness in order to help with your anxiety.

Regardless of identifying your triggers, you may need to take a deeper look at the root causes of anxiety in your life.

One of the best ways to become more aware of your anxiety and begin dealing with them is to become more self-aware.

Self-awareness is important, yet difficult because it is all about examining your actions and behaviors that cause you to react the way you do. You have to look at your past behaviors and your present behavior to understand how you can change your actions. Self-awareness is also difficult because we tend to have a bias about our actions. Let's face it. We think we are the greatest thing since sliced bread. Do not get me wrong. It is great to have self-esteem about who we are, but it is more important to be realistic about our opportunities for improvement in order to carve out the best life possible for ourselves. Being self-aware brings on a bevy of benefits. When you are self-aware, you are able to be more empathetic and compassionate to everyone that you meet instead of just being blinded by your ignorance and personal biases. Self-aware people are able to relate to a variety of people because they are open-minded and able to adjust their emotions to someone despite their own inherent biases and prejudices. Self-aware people do have biases, but they are able to identify those biases. Self-aware people are not blindsided by their prejudices to the point where they can't understand where their feeling they may have is coming from. Self-aware people know their strengths and weaknesses and are open-minded and fair. However, they do not get this way unless they have a heart-to-heart with themselves.

The first thing you need to do before you have this conversation is to set aside a day for yourself. Make sure that you will not be interrupted because this will be one of the most difficult conversations that you will have. You can bring tissue, pen, and paper. You can have your computer nearby, if necessary, to keep notes digitally. You can also buy a journal if you prefer to keep notes by hand without having to deal with individual pieces of paper. You can even have an empowering music playlist because you may need it. Give permission to yourself to feel every emotion that you may experience with no judgement then go ahead and buckle your proverbial seat-belt. There are no other people who can have this conversation with you.

The first topic of discussion you want to have with yourself is figuring out what personality type you are. There are lots of personality online assessments that are free, easy and quick to take that gives you insight about your personality. On the piece of paper, what are your initial thoughts of who you are? Are you hot tempered? Are you level-headed and cool or are you a mixture of both? Whatever you are thinking about it and then take an assessment test. One of the most popular personality tests is the Jung and Briggs Myers typology test or the Predictive Index. However, there are other ones that you can try out if you prefer.

After taking the test, you will next want to ask yourself a series of questions:

Values

- Who is the person that you admire the most? What is it that you admire about them?
- What character traits do you love about yourself? This does not have to be related to emotional intelligence. It can be something that makes you feel great about yourself.

- What character traits do you love about others? What are those traits that you wish you had?
- What do you consider your core values to be? Think about these values from a spiritual, emotional, mental, physical and financial perspective.
- Who is the person I want to be? Think about the legacy you want to leave. Who will people say that you were when you leave this world?
- What do you think your purpose in life is? For some people, this consists of who you want to help and how you want to help them. They take into account what activities they like to do and activities they do not like to do when making this decision.
- How would you rate your self-esteem on a scale of 1-10, with 10 being the highest?
- How are you working on your self-esteem? What daily habits are you forming to make sure that your self-esteem is high and you will not be susceptible to bad decisions?
- Am I working on becoming that person daily?
- What are your strengths? What things are easy for you and what things do other people say you are good at?
- What are your weaknesses? In other words, what are areas that you can improve upon? Weaknesses are also known as areas or opportunities.
- What daily habits are making your weaknesses worse?
- What daily habits are improving your strengths?
- How would your closest friends and family members describe you?
- Do people, especially your friends and family, typically

tell you the truth or what you want to hear? Do they think you are sensitive and tend to hedge how they tell you the truth? Or are they very blunt with you and are not afraid to hurt your feelings if you need to know the truth?

- On a scale of 1 to 10, how would you describe your communication skills? Why would you describe it that way? Give three examples.
- On a scale of 1 to 10, how you describe your communication skills when you are angry, stressed or arguing? Give three examples of why you feel that way.
- When do you typically analyze your successful days or successful days to see why they were successful? If you do not, come up with a time when you should start doing that.
- What do you do when you accomplish your goals or are happy? Does your celebratory behavior turn into negative habits?
- When do you typically analyze your horrible days and failures to see why it went wrong and what you can do to improve it?
- How often do you seek out constructive criticism that can help you improve? Who do you go to when you need to get constructive criticism? If you don't have anyone, who could you go to?
- What is your spiritual outlook in life? Go more into detail. What are your views about the afterlife?
- What do you feel when someone you know is success-ful? Are you generally happy for them or do you tend

to get jealous? Think about the why behind your behavior. This will help you develop more trends.

- What do you feel when someone you know fails? Are you happy with glee? Do you feel like you are in competition with them?

Once you go through all of these questions, have a conversation you would like to have is with someone you trust. Ask them "*do they agree with the results of the personality test?*" and with the answers to the above questions that you asked yourself. The trick is to ask someone who will be honest with you, yet tactful and constructive. You may be surprised that the way you value or think about yourself is not how other people look at you at all. Be sure to take what they say with a grain of salt because they have their bias as well. When you are listening to other people, do not get defensive. Be quiet. The only thing you should say to them is thank you. Combining your personality assessment results plus feedback from other people plus what your thoughts are you will be able to get a clearer view of if you are the person that you think you are.

The next conversation you need to have with yourself is to figure out what types of things make you upset, cause you stress or anxiety. On your piece of paper, draw four lines to create 5 columns. At the top of the first column, write "*Triggers*". At the top of the second column, write "*Reactions*". At the top of the third column, write '*How Do I Feel?*' At the top of the fourth column, write, '*How Would I Like To React?*' Then on the last column, write '*Steps I'm Taking.*' Then brainstorm. What things push your buttons? Is it when somebody chews with their mouth open? Is it when someone pops their gum?

Is it when someone tells you directions from the passenger seat? Whatever the trigger that upsets you, write it down on the left side.

Questions you can consider when thinking about your reactions:

- Do you blow up? Do you tend to yell and scream or say bad words?
- Do you just ignore what is bothering you until you blow up? Do you avoid expressing how you feel and find yourself blowing up before it's too late?
- Are you able to address the issue constructively? Are you able to be calm and solution-focused?
- How do you feel about your normal reaction?
- Do you think it is getting the job done or do you find yourself still frustrated?
- When you try to confront someone about the situation, are you doing it gracefully or are you being confrontational? Do you yell and scream or do you find that you are normally calm?

Now that you know what your trigger is and how you typically react, how would you like to react? Would you like to be more graceful? Would you like to ignore insignificant things that bother you? Once you add that, consider how you feel about these reactions? Do you think there is work you can do on your reactions? Do you feel like you are doing ok? Lastly, figure out a way to better manage your reactions by the expectations that you would. By knowing what your triggers are you can better handle how you react to those things.

This type of deep reflection is an important way for you to become more self-aware. It also helps you create a stress-management system to handle things that may stress you out and cause you anxiety. What are you going to do when you are stressed? Take the time to create that system now so you are effectively handling your stress.

If you've made it this far, great job! We have more introspecting to do, so go ahead and buckle your seatbelt. This is where things can get ugly. The nature of being self-aware is one of introspection and honesty even when it is uncomfortable. You have to take an intense look into your past in order to figure out where you're going in the future. So now we are going to take a deep look into your past.

The first thing you want to consider is what are the very best memories you have from your earliest memory to the present time? Then think about what are the very worst memories that you have from the earliest memory to the present time? Please take your time when writing these memories down and go in as much detail as possible. This is essentially a written record of who you are. Next, you need to think about the conclusions that you drew from those memories? What are the results and conclusions that you have from those memories about life? Do these conclusions help you make judgments about people or about life in general? For example, if you had a cousin that only kept Tootsie Tolls and threw all other lollipops out, does that affect why you only like Tootsie Tolls now? Do you think Tootsie Roll lollipops are horrible without ever having a Tootsie Roll lollipop yourself so you are unable to conclusively make a judgment about whether you like Tootsie Roll lollipops or not?

After you have your memories down and the conclusions you've gained from those memories, now you have to dig deeper. It is time to make two columns. Title this page, 'My Beliefs.' At the top of the left column, write, 'Healthy Beliefs.' At the top of the right column, write 'Limiting Beliefs.' Next review the list of conclusions from your memories and put the appropriate belief in the proper corresponding column. Which ones are healthy? Which ones are limiting you?

A limiting belief is a belief that is not necessarily true, but one that you believe based on experiences that have shaped your views. An example of a limiting belief would be that if you need to get healthy, but you see that no one in your family is healthy, you may believe that being healthy is not a big deal since no one in your family takes health seriously. Thus, you feel that being healthy is underrated, and this limiting belief hinders you from seeking a healthier lifestyle. Limiting beliefs do not have to be just about negative beliefs. Sometimes limiting beliefs can be positive, but also hinder you. For example, lots of people have the limiting belief, that 'The love of money is the root of all evil.' which in turn causes them to have negative thoughts about money. They think if they make a lot of money, they will be evil so they do not seek out opportunities to make money which in turn would improve their life. Even though it is good advice that loving money too much can be evil, it is a limiting belief when taking it out of context and hindering one's growth.

As you examine your memories, ask yourself questions about these memories:

• Did we play a role in any of these memories? Do we

need to take responsibility for any of these actions? Try to look at the situation objectively like you are a bird viewing the situation from a bird's eye point-of-view

- Can you fill any personal needs without destructive behavior? You can do everything in moderation. But are you doing anything in excess?
- Am I living for today or am I stuck in the past trying to fix any of these memories? Sometimes the past can weigh us down. It is good to see the past as a way to enlighten your future behaviors but not to the point of your past limiting your future happiness.
- Is there anything that I can improve to proactively handle any of these situations in the future? If you notice any negative trends or cycles from your memories, how can you stop them and turn those negative cycles into positive cycles?
- Do I need to step out my comfort zone? Am I stuck in my ways? Do I need to eat at new restaurants, be around different people or travel some to open myself up to new experiences? When you go to the restaurant, do you order the same thing every single time? This one should be pretty easy to answer, but another big clue if people tell you that you are stuck in your ways.

While examining the conclusions you may have about your memories, you may also realize that you have some forgiving and forgetting to do. You may need to call someone and ask them for their forgiveness. No matter how big or small, make note of the trends you see in your conclusions and be honest with yourself about how these memories are affecting you now. Be mindful that if you need to speak to someone, and they are not receptive of your experience, that's ok. Say what you need to say and move on. Try your hardest to make peace with the painful memories. In the midst of this activity, you may also realize that you need to set boundaries. Boundaries are important because they help you figure out how to handle people. Boundaries may even help you deal with your anxiety better because you are limiting things that cause you anxiety. If you know that certain people are not good, make a boundary to not be around them. If you know that during a certain time of the month, certain things piss you off more than other things, set yourself up for success and create the necessary hedges around you. At this point, if you notice you may want to talk to a therapist to do more work on these memories, do not hesitate to find one and set an appointment.

Doing this activity may stir up lots of emotions and that's okay. If at any point, you need to take a step back, feel free to do so. Then come back. The most important thing to remember is that your emotions or feelings are important. They are how you feel about a particular situation. Be kind to yourself and non-judgmental about these feelings.

The next thing we need to consider that can be contributing to your stress is your daily activities. Please keep track of your daily activities in your journal. You can print off an online schedule and fill it in if you need to. When you're filling in your schedule, make sure that you are tracking your energy levels, sleep patterns and what you're eating, as well. Questions you can ask would be:

• What time of the day are you doing your best work?

Think about when you are most productive. What other factors do you notice contribute to your productivity? Is it when you have peace and quiet and your kids are not around or is it when it is loud and chaos around you. This is specific to your personality.

- Is this time consistent or does it change? Another great trend to notice when answering this question is to think about the moon. Are you most productive when it is a full moon or at another time?

- What time of day are you not doing your best work? Knowing when you are not productive will help you not schedule productive activities during that time. For some people who are morning owls, any time in the night does not work them. For others, the afternoons just do not work, and other people prefer to midnight oil.

- Is this time the same or does it change?

- What activities are draining me during the day? Do you exercise or hang out with exhausting people? Think of all the things that tend to deplete your energy levels.

- What activities are giving me energy? Do you notice if you have a certain schedule that it gives you energy? Do you notice when you are around other people who do not procrastinate that it helps? Make an exhaustive list.

- Do I notice any difference in my energy levels depending on the foods I eat? Do you have more energy when you only eat certain foods? Do caffeine and sugar cause you to crash often? Does meat cause your stomach to hurt? Does eating a heavy lunch fuel you for the rest of the day?

- Am I getting enough sleep daily? For most people, 8 hours is recommended, but other can get ways with anything form 5-7 hours. When do you notice that you are most productive?
- Am I happy most days? Or am I miserable most days? How would you say that you feel generally? Do you feel that you are living in your purpose?

When you make a note of what you are doing everyday can only help you deal with your anxiety better. You are taking account of the things in your life and openly examining trends about when you are getting anxiety and what could possible be causing it. To better manage your anxiety, you must get into the habit of meditating or journaling. You can journal or meditate digitally with an app or with old-school methods like a journal, pen, and paper.

An easy template to use when reflecting on your days, helps you stay focused on being the person you want to be includes five simple questions:

- Did I learn anything to do? If so, what? Try to be as detailed as possible.
- Did anything go bad today? If so, what? Try to be as detailed as possible.
- What did I do that was nice for myself today? Did you say kind words to yourself for doing a job well done or anything that would boost your self-esteem?
- What went great today? What things did you do really well today?
- Is there anything I can do to make tomorrow better

than today? Be specific and list a way that you can make tomorrow better than today. If the day was a phenomenal day, you can write ways you can make the next day just as good at the day.

You should also consider whether you should start meditating or journaling? To being journaling, find a journal and just free right about everything that bothers you. By doing the work of freewriting, you're able to write about anything that's bothering you. You are in charge of your destiny. The great thing about journaling is that you have a record of your emotions. You can notice patterns and trends in your behavior to see what makes your anxious, depressed or happy.

Becoming self-aware is hard, but necessary, especially if you want to deal with your anxiety better.

This last section will give you quick tips to help you manage your anxiety easier, along with journaling.

- Be Honest With Yourself About Identifying Your Triggers – Honesty isn't always fun, but it is necessary. Do the work and be open to examining the cause of your triggers so that you can manage them better.
- Don't Be Afraid To Seek Help – Speaking with a trained professional is key to helping you tackle your anxiety. You can do wonders by working through your triggers and a professional would be more than willing to help.
- Journal or get a workbook – Reading this book shows that you are on the right track! Don't be afraid to use it as a resource.

- Find a support group online or in person – Don't underestimate the power of having someone you can talk to.
- Manage your expectations – Instead of focusing on what could be, embrace what actually is. Being more mindful will help you be more accepting of your life situation, no matter what's going on.
- Eat and sleep healthier – A healthy lifestyle can do wonders for your anxiety. Do not neglect your body.
- Avoid taking things personally. – When we see ourselves as a constant victim, we can cause anxiety. Let your victimhood go and watch your anxiety go with it.

4

Beginning Your Mindfulness Practice

How often does it feel like life is racing by? We often do not have the time to take the time and smell the roses. We often do not take the time to truly embrace our loved ones just to hug without feeling like we have to rush off to the next thing. In this social media frenzy of a world, we live in today, it is easy to lose focus. As a result, if we are not careful, we can easily move like a zombie in our day-to-day lives without full experiencing everyday life. Thankfully, when you begin to practice mindfulness for just a few moments per day, you will find that you will become more open to the full experiences of live and our daily activities will slow down. And we may, shall I daresay, begin to enjoy life for yourself and enjoy thriving relationships with others to the point that life becomes enjoyable. Yes, mindfulness meditation is a seriously powerful tool that can change your life, but it is also fun! And guess what the fun part is?

The fun part about being a mindfulness meditation practitioner is actually doing mindfulness meditation. Before you begin to meditate, a few ground rules need to be set. Also, a few things should be given as a reminder, too. First thing, when you are being mindful, remember that you are being mindful about something in the present time. The second thing is that for our practice, we will be using our breaths as the center of mindfulness. The more you become aware of what is going on around you and are able to use your breaths to center you, the easier you will be able to experience mindfulness. Becoming mindful can help you break through any biased perceptions you may have, and it may make you feel uncomfortable at times. However, if you are able to make it through the discomfort, you will be able to enjoy if fully. Also, remember, mindfulness does not judge your thoughts or focus on any bias that you may have. It just notes your thoughts as they pass by in your mind until you are able to just let the thoughts be. Your thoughts are not good or bad. You are merely a video recording nothing but what you see. Mindfulness helps you experience real time in super sharp focus. The more you dedicate to focusing on being mindful, the more your mindfulness muscle will be developed, and the easier doing mindfulness meditation will become

The very first thing you should do before practicing mindfulness meditation is to set a pin in your busy schedule that's going to be dedicated to your meditation practice. This is very important. When you set this time, please be consistent. Make sure that this time is distraction free with no person or task able to distract or interrupt you. If you need to set an alarm to remind you, do so. If you need to set your phone on do not disturb, do so. It is important for you to take this seriously if you want to get good at it. To help you set yourself up for success, stick to the time you want and do not let anything get in your way.

When you first begin, it is normal that you may feel a bit weird. Hence, to help you acclimate to the process faster, try to meditate more than one time per day. You can try to have a meditation session at least two times a day. To help make the transition easier, you can try to meditate at the same time every day, but if you aren't able to do that it is okay. Worst case scenario, on that day you want to meditate, but you are unable to, try to make up the time that you missed. If you absolutely have no time to spare in your super-jam-packed schedule, you can try to meditate while doing another activity. If this is the route you must take, when you are doing the other activity, focus on doing the activity and make note of the thoughts that pass through your mind while you are meditating. For example, you can try to meditate while cooking. When you meditate while doing an activity, make sure that you are doing the activity for its value, not for some other end. For example, if you are cooking, you are cooking because cooking is an activity, not because you begrudgingly have to cook for your family. Another time people like to meditate is while driving, especially if they have a long commute. Just be careful not to get too relaxed that you lose focus behind the wheel!

Another way to ease into your meditation practice is if you start off meditating in 5-10 minutes increments, at least twice a day, then work to increase your time. If you are having a difficult time even with the 5-10 minutes, you can start off by dedicating just 60 seconds a day and build from there. If you find the 60 seconds challenging, cut it down to 30 seconds and build from there. I cannot stress the importance of whatever you select, commit to it, because if you are able to commit at least 11 days of mediation, your mindfulness meditation habit is more likely to stick than if you did not do at least 11 days.

Something else to consider before you set your time is to consider the time of day that you want to meditate. For some, doing an early morning session sets the tone for the rest of your day. If they can meditate in the morning, they find that the rest of their day goes smoothly. They experience less anxiety and frustration. They remain calm and peaceful throughout the day. For others, the best time to meditate is not in the morning, but the reverse time. Some find that when they meditate after a long day of work, they can decompress from the day's stress and be set up to begin a brand-new day. When they meditate at night, they can sleep better because they are more relaxed and have put their stress to the side. Others still prefer to meditate in the mid-day. This allows them to settle down from the hustle bustle of the day and then prepare them to finish the rest of the day out strong. They also find that a quick afternoon meditation session reinvigorates them and gives them a much-needed energy boost in a much healthier way than eating sugar or drinking caffeine. Not to mention they do not experience any crashes either. I suggest trying every time to see which time is better. If you want to take your practice to the next level, commit to meditating at least twice a day to see how that affects you.

The second step you want to do before you begin meditating is to find the place where you will be meditating. When you find the place, hook it up or customize the place to your liking. For greater comfort, while meditating, you can consider purchasing a meditation pillow to sit on or lie on. If you want to save money, you can use what you have around the house, like comfy pillows that you already have around. You can use a comfortable blanket or shaggy rug, as well. Once you select your place, you will also want to make sure that the place is free of distractions. If there is a computer or television or tablet or phone nearby, be sure to put it out of your sight so you cannot be distracted by it. If there is a place to plug your phone in nearby, do not charge your phone in your meditation place. I guarantee you that when you begin to meditate your phone will become a hug distraction. The saying 'Out of sight, out of mind' is definitely true! When you are selecting your room, consider the placement of the room in relation to your house and outside. You want the room to be quiet. There's nothing more distracting than trying to meditate and you have a huge noise to overcome, like an ambulance or fire truck passing in the background. Sometimes it is impossible to eliminate noise completely but try to eliminate as much noise as you can. In your meditation room, make sure that the room temperature is comfortable for you. You do not want it too hot that you're uncomfortable and sweating or too hot that it makes you groggy. You also do not want the room temperature too cold that you are unable to move your fingers and toes.

Once you have your time selected, and your special place decorated to your liking, it is time to meditate. On the day that you want to meditate, you want to figure out the best position that you want to be in throughout the session. One of the most popular poses is called the lotus pose. It is an advanced yoga pose and requires some flexibility. It is the one pose you most often see people in when they are meditating. Before you begin, you will want to stretch. To get into lotus pose, you'll want to be seated on the floor and have your spine straight. Let your arms rest by your side. Then you will want to bend your right knee and bring it to your chest. Then, drop your right ankle on the crease in your left hip so your right foot sole is facing the sky. The top of your foot should be resting on your hip crease. Next, do the same thing on the other side. Bend your left knee and put your left ankle on top of your right shin so your left ankle is crossed over the top of your right shin. Your left foot sole should also be facing upwards and the top of your ankle and foot should be resting on your right hip crease.

Once you are in this position, bring your knees in to your body as close as possible while sitting as straight as possible. Your groin should also be as flat and close to the ground as possible. You'll want to put your hands on your knees with your palms facing up. Then create a circle with your thumb and index finger and leave the rest of your fingers extended. Lotus pose can be challenging for those with limited flexibility or those who are just beginning to do yoga. The good thing is that there are other positions you can try using if Lotus Pose is a challenge for you. You are able to sit on the floor with your knees bent and legs crossed over each other. You can also just sit in a chair or lie down. The most important thing is to find a position that is comfortable for you.

Once your time is determined, your space is ready, and your position is selected, it is time to begin meditating. When you are in the most comfortable position possible, try to let your body feel loose. You can do this by rolling your neck and arms and shoulders in a circle. You can also stretch the muscles in your face by making a full smile and then a half smile. As you get loose, if you have any tension feel it roll away. Next, you'll want to make sure that your posture is top-notch. Keep your back and neck as straight as possible. Try to keep your stomach relaxed. To take your posture up another level, you can tilt your chin down slightly. Using the correct postures will allow your breaths to be as deep as possible and you will be able to draw in deeper breaths. After your posture is checked, you can then figure out what to do with your hands if you are not doing lotus pose. Your hands can rest on top of your lap, to the side of you on the floor or on top of one another on your knees with your palms up. The next decision you have to make is to decide what to do with your eyes. You can decide to keep them open, half-closed or closed completely. If you decide to keep them closed, be sure not to fall asleep when you are meditating. If you are afraid you may fall asleep, it may be best to keep your eyes open or at least half-open.

Next, focus on your breathing. First, just observe your breath. Remember, breathing is the key to helping you concentrate throughout the meditation exercise. As you breathe, you can notice your chest going up and down. Breathe in through your nose and exhale through your mouth. It is totally ok to breathe through your mouth if you have to. Once you have observed your breath, you can then begin to count your breaths. When you breathe in through your nose and then exhale through your mouth, count it as one breath cycle. Try to count to 5, which would be five completed breath cycles of inhaling an exhaling. Then try to get to 10 with your breath cycles. It should go like this: Inhale-one. Exhale - two. Inhale – three. Exhale- four. If any thought interrupts you, start the count over again until you are able to reach 10 complete breath cycles. This is a wonderful breathing exercise to do when you begin. Now, remember, you are just starting so it may be difficult to retain your concentration and that's ok. Be patient, kind and gentle with yourself. If you do find yourself losing focus, the most important thing is to get back on focus as soon as you lose focus by concentrating on your breaths. Keep practicing this until you are able to count to 10 breath cycles with ease.

Then the next step to take your breathing to the next level is to begin counting your inhales and exhales as 1 complete breath cycle. So it would look like this: Inhale – one. Exhale – one. Inhale – two. Exhale – two. So on and so forth until you are able to reach 10 with ease. Once you are able to do that, then you can begin to focus on your breath only. This may take a while, and that's ok. You also may have trouble completing focusing on your breath, and that's ok as well. If you have a thought to interrupt your concentration on your breathing, observe the thought and then begin to count again. The easier you are able to control your breath, the easier your mindfulness meditation will be. Then you can start meditating while doing other activities until mindfulness just become part of your daily life.

So, what happens if you are unable to still your mind? That's ok. Keep practicing until you get better. What happens if you are unable to sit in the lotus position? That's ok as well. Find the most comfortable position for you and then go from there. What if I'm unable to be nonjudgmental with thoughts that arise? Guess what? This will take time as well. As long as you are dedicated to improving your meditation practice every time you do it, you are making progress. The more you do it the easier it will be. This is a lifelong commitment so do not feel like you have to be perfect starting out.

This chapter has given you a wide overview of how to get started with mindfulness meditation. As a recap, before you begin your mindfulness meditation practice, make sure that you have already committed to a consistent time that you will meditate in order to build your practice. Try to start off at least five minutes twice a day for at least 11 days so you can build a habit. Once your time is selected, you will want to make sure your special mediation place is specific to you and your needs and most importantly, free of all distractions. There are a variety of positions you can take when meditating, just be sure to choose one that is most comfortable for you, whether it be lotus pose, sitting down, lying down, or standing. When you do begin to meditate, focus on your breathing. Be non-judgmental about thoughts that may float by. If you do find yourself being distracted, bring your attention back to your breathing. More importantly, be gentle with yourself and remember that the more you practice, the better you will become. I know you still may have a few questions about mindfulness so the next section should help clear up concerns you may have by giving you the answers to popular questions you may have.

<u>I have trouble clearing my mind when I meditate. Is it a necessity that when I meditate for my mind to be completely clear?</u>

No, having a completely clear mind is not a necessity before you begin to meditate. Mindfulness meditation helps you to see your thoughts more clearly. Your thoughts are supposed to trickle along in your mind instead of racing by. Think of mindfulness meditation as allowing your thoughts to go by like a weather scan. They can change minute by minute or hour by hour. Your meditation practice allows you to be in tune with your thoughts. It allows you to keep a pulse on how your thoughts change.

<u>I'm not good at yoga. Will I still be able to do mindfulness meditation?</u>

Sure thing! Mindfulness meditation encourages people to get in a comfortable position before they meditate. For some that may be a popular yoga pose like the lotus pose, but that is not a requirement. Other lie down or sit in a comfortable position. Whatever is the most comfortable position for you is the position that you should use. Also, while mindfulness meditation encourages you to be still, there are lots of moving meditation like yoga or tai chi or mindfulness of walking that encourages movement while you meditate if you ever want to build on your mindfulness meditation practice.

<u>Will mindfulness meditation clear all my problems instantly?</u>

Great question. Mindfulness meditation is not a quick fix.

Its power lies in the ability to locate thought patterns and behaviors that may be problematic for you. If you have certain health problems, mindfulness meditation is a great way to cope, but if your symptoms continue to persist, you may need to check in with a doctor for further suggestions for treatment. Mindfulness meditation may not totally eliminate your stress, anxiety or depression, but it will help you cope and manage the situation a lot better than if you were not meditating and certainly without the use of medication.

Is mindfulness only for those who practice a certain religion?

No. You can be any religion and practice mindfulness meditation. It does draw from the Buddhist tradition, but just because you practice mindfulness does not make you a Buddhist, just like drinking wine does not make you a Christian. The great thing about mindfulness meditation is that it can fit in your lifestyle no matter if you are religious or not. If you are interested in adding more Buddhist elements to your practice, feel free to learn more and incorporate it into your mindfulness meditation journey.

Is not mindfulness just dealing with positive thinking?

Mindfulness meditation encourages non-judgmental positive thinking when examining your thoughts, but it does not run away from negative thoughts. Mindfulness meditation also encourages the examination of neutral feelings as well. When you meditate and negative thoughts occur, it is encouraged that you examine the thought and try to figure out where it came from and why you think that way as a way to be able to handle any situation you may find yourself in-whether that situation is positive or negative.

How long will it take me to learn mindfulness meditation?

The journey to learn how to meditation has no set schedule. Learning how to do mindfulness meditation can actually be quite linear. One day you may do well and feel like you're moving forward another day, you may feel like you are going nowhere. One day you will be able to do all the exercises correctly, and the next day you may run into trouble. It is more important to be consistent when you meditate so you can feel comfortable and improve your practice for you to receive the benefits.

5

Anxiety Mindfulness Meditation

"To think in terms of either pessimism or optimism oversimplifies the truth. The problem is to see reality as it is." –
Thích Nhất Hạnh

<u>Dealing With Your Day-to-Day Anxieties Writing Prompt</u>

1. How would you describe your current reality? How can you improve it?
2. How are you currently coping with your anxiety in your day-to-day life?
3. What can you do to rid yourself of the biggest trigger you are having?
4. What is one breathing technique you will do today to help deal with your anxiety?

5. What is one relaxation technique you will do today to help deal with your anxiety?

6. What one thing will you do today to make it a success?

Mindfulness Meditation Script For Anxiety #1

Collect your scrambled thoughts one by one. Put them in a basket of forgetfulness. Tuck the basket away for the time being. Breathe in and breathe out while you collect your thoughts. Steadily slow your breaths down until you can only feel your body fill with the positive reassurance from every deep breath that you take.

Be still. Be calm. For the next 10 seconds, be completely at peace.

Look at the blank canvas of your mind. Think of situations that cause you anxiety. Do you see the vivid colors that are splashing on your mental canvas?

Feel your breath steady the white canvas. Exhale any thought and colors that may be coming to paint that canvas. Exhale and push them away until your mental canvas is totally blank.

Inhale slowly. Exhale slowly. Inhale forgiveness. Exhale anger.

You are the master of calm. The painter of calmness in your life. Breath slowly and deeply. Each breath steadies your mind's frantic thoughts. Keep the canvas as white as possible.

With every negative thought that wants to overcome your white canvas of calm, dump feelings of forgives and understanding and compassion and forgetfulness until the canvas is back white again.

Embrace the difficulty of trying to still your thoughts.

Keep stilling your thoughts. When every thought of anxiety pops up, run your broad brush or love across it.

Feel the power of your breaths guiding your hands and helping you keep your brush steady. Helping you paint with steady fingers and kind heats and kind minds. Feel your body being reinforced by the positivity of your breaths empowering you to say all the right things that need to be said and to take all the right actions that need to be taken.

Do you see how white and bright your mental canvas is? Now splash kindness, understanding, gratitude, and love on the canvas. Keep your mental canvas with you. Know that you can return to this canvas to start over at any time.

Open your eyes and keep your mental picture with you.

<u>Mindfulness Meditation For Anxiety #2</u>

We will begin our mindfulness meditation for anxiety right now. If you are experiencing anxiety currently or have been experiencing it for a while, I know it is not the best feeling in the world. You may be hurting. You may be scared, but know that you're going to be okay. I know it is hard for you to believe this right now, but know that the responses your body is giving to your anxiety are going to be over soon.

Know that relief from your anxiety is coming. It does not last forever. You want to know why? It is because your body has a built-in stress relief already. Your body will naturally deal with anxiety on its own terms. So keep this gem in the back of your mind and know that your body is always helping you deal with your anxiety. It is up to you to activate the stress-relief by being relaxed. It is up to you to help your body relax by taking in deep breaths. The inhales are going to help calm your body. The purpose of this meditation is to use your breathing in order to relax.

You may feel like it is difficult to breathe but be aware that your body is already breathing. Listen to your breath right now. If your breaths are short, try to lengthen your breath by breathing to the count of three. Breathe in for a cycle of three counts; 1, 2, 3. Then breathe out for a breath cycle of three: 1, 2, 3. Notice your heartbeat. Notice if it is going fast or slow.

Let's try to slow your breathing down. Breathe in again. This time we are going to hold the breath cycle for 5 counts. Breathe in 1,2,3,4,5. Then breathe out: 1,2,3,4,5.

Breathe in deeply again. Now breathe out like you're blowing a birthday cake with a lot of candles. You want to make sure that you are blowing each and every one of those candles out. Breathe in and hold your breath in for three counts: 1,2,3. Now breathe out slowly: 1,2,3. Keep this up. You're doing a great job.

For extra support, you can hold up your fingers and pretend they are the candles in front of you. Now blow the air out open your mouth and make a slight sound as you blow it out. Make a gentle 'hoo' sounds as you let your breath out. You can do this breath cycle one more time, or you can continue to breathe slowly and gently.

Be aware of your body. See how your body is controlling your breathing? Do you see how your body makes sure that it is getting enough air? Do you see how your body wants to help you calm down? In your comfortable position, close your eyes again and take it all in. Take in how awesome and self-sufficient your body is and how you can help it.

You may still feel overwhelmed. You may feel like no one

is with you right now, but know that you are enough. You are your breathing. Your breath is a wave. With every deep inhale you give, the higher the wave is. Ride the wave as high as you can. Breathe in and let your breath out with a big whoosh.

If you want to feel more comfortable, feel free to turn the light off or stand up and pace around as you continue with this breathing. If these steps do not help, know that your anxiety will continue to decrease on its own. You can continue to help your anxiety decrease by breathing. The more you breathe, the calmer you will be. Take it slow. Imagine with that feeling of calm feels like. Is it blue or yellow or white? Is it vivid, pastel, or bold? Feel that the deeper you breathe, the more you relax and the faster your anxiety will go.

As you breathe, feel that is helping your body to relax. With each breath, you breathe in, breathe in deeply and feel your body getting calmer. Please try and focus on your breath right now.

You do not have to worry about what is triggering you or causing you anxiety. You do not have to worry about what you're going to do to deal with the anxiety. The only thing you should focus on is your breathing. Feel the flutter of the clothing against your chest every time you breathe in and breathe out. If you're feeling uncomfortable, and you need to find a more comfortable position do so gently but continue to focus on your breath.

You are going to be okay. I know it doesn't feel like it, but you are going to be okay. Now we want to feel the warmth that's associated with calm. You can warm your hands together gently until you feel your palm slightly warming up.

Do not go vigorously - go smoothly, slowly, and gently. Do you feel the warmth?

Now that you can focus on your hands moving, how does it sound? That sound can help you ground yourself from your anxiety and sent to you along with your breathing. When you feel that you focused on your hands enough, you can stop and place your hands by your side and breath in again.

Relax and know that anxiety is normal. Focus on the sensations of your body. Notice how they're different from when you first began. Listen to the sound your breath makes as you breathe in and you breathe out. Moment by moment, the breath is helping you pass this level of anxiety.

Anxiety is a natural process. It is not always easy to feel, but it is natural. Help your body react by continuing to breathe. Do not have any judgment about your state of mind right now. Know that life happens. But when you're able to be in this moment, just like now, with your breath, you can focus on the good. You can focus on just being. You do not have to make a decision to do anything. Just be here right now with your breath and your body. Know that you're going to be okay.

Accept your body for what it is. Accept your brain for what it gives you. Accept your responses for what they are because they are what they are. affirmations to help you and your body recover. You can either listen and continue to breathe slowly or you can repeat them after with every breath.

Breathe in, and then breathe out. Repeat after me. "I accept who I am no matter what I am feeling." The past does not determine who I am, nor the future. The only thing that matters is the right now and by accepting who you are now, you are being mindful.

Breathe in, and then breathe out. Repeat after me. "I know that anxiety does not last forever. My anxiety will pass." Anxiety feels like it will last forever, but if you take it in the present moment, you will be able to ride the wave to calmness.

Breathe in, and then breathe out. Repeat after me. "My body is prepared to handle my anxiety. I can help by breathing." Be grateful and know that your body can handle any stress that it faces. The most important thing is to help your body out by breathing deeply.

Know that deep down inside, that as each second goes by and as every minute goes by, I feel my anxiety going away. And I feel a large dose of calm replacing it.

Repeat after me. "I feel relaxed. I am more comfortable." As you continue to breathe, notice how the breath is affecting your body.

Breathe in, and then breathe out. Repeat after me. "I accept how I feel right now. I am calm. I'm going to be okay. I am relaxed. I am at peace." Keep breathing. You will continue to feel your body come down from the anxiety that you are experiencing. Pay careful attention to how your body feels in a relaxed state.

Great job. Notice how you feel. Continue to feel relaxed. Continue to breathe in and breathe out. Notice how loose your limbs feel. Notice how easy your breaths come and go. Notice how easy it is for your body to pick up on the next breath after you breathe one.

Continue to relax for as long as you want. You can

continue to stay in your comfortable position and breathe in and breathe out, or you can go ahead and bring the meditation to an end. Whatever you feel like doing, be mindful of the decision.

On the count of three, this meditation will be ending. You can replay this guided meditation again if you need to or continue to breathe deeply and silently on your own. One. Two. Three.

6

Social Anxiety
Mindfulness Meditation

"When we get too caught up in the busyness of the world, we lose connection with one another – and ourselves." –
Jack Kornfield

1. Connection with people is an important human need. When we lose connection with others, it can affect us. What causes you anxiety about your connection with other people? In what ways have you lost that connection with others?
2. How are you currently coping with your social anxiety?
3. What three coping technique, whether breathing, relaxation or self-reflection will you do to help with your social anxiety today?

4. What is one way you will work on overcoming your social anxiety today?

<u>Mindfulness Meditation for Social Anxiety #1</u>

Get comfortable and close your eyes.

Today is a wonderful day. It is a beautiful day.

For one moment, listen to the chirp of the birds. Listen to the sound of the cars passing by. Focus on the chirp until you no longer hear it. Focus on the sound of the car as it passes by and you can no longer hear the rumbling of its motor. Listen to the silence. Feel the stillness in the silence. Embrace the stillness. The stillness is you.

Focus on your breathing. Feel the gentle rise of your chest going up and down softly. Notice the thumping of your heart. Breathe in slowly and deeply, take in all the great news you are going to receive today. When you inhale, feel all the positive energy spreading throughout every nerve and cell of your body.

Exhale any negative thoughts you may have had today. Exhale all of the negative energy from miscommunication that you may be having. Maybe you are thinking negative thoughts that prevent you from seeing that people are just people. Let go of your lofty expectations of others.

Inhale the grace that you want others to give to you. Let that grace affect every part of your being so you can be gracious. Inhale positive thoughts that will help you speak the exact right thing that you need to say. Inhale the possibilities of gentle words and the power they have.

Exhale all of the bad things that are not going to happen. They have disappeared. They are no longer there. Inhale all of the positive, amazing, great things that are going to happen to you today.

Know that you are loved, and this is your day. Inhale the goodness of the day. Inhale the possibilities that today could be the very best day of your life. This is the day that will start a domino chain effect of nothing but good things to come for yourself and for others.

Open your eyes and brave the day

Mindfulness Meditation For Social Anxiety #2

Start this meditation by settlings and reflecting of one kind thing you have done recently for someone. Bring your thoughts to that one moment where you gave selflessly.

Imagine how you felt. Now shift your attention to something someone has done nicely for you. Breathe deep and purposefully. Receive the life force equipping you with the spirit of kindness.

Breathe out any mean thought you have had to even the smallest create. Breathe in the spirit of kindness. Breathe in as much kindness as you can. You are kind to spiders, ants, and ladybugs.

You are kind to strangers you pass by in the street and your friends and family members that you love deeply. You are kind to that one person in the office that no one speaks to. You are kind to the child who is having a hard time at home. You are kind to someone at the exact perfect time who needed to have someone to be kind to them. You are their last hope in humanity. Embrace the gravity that being kind has.

Breathe out your knee-jerk reactions to rude people. Breathe and reinforce yourself with the spirit of kindness to even the meanest person you know. They are really in need of your kindness. Breathe out how you want to act to them. Breathe in the spirit of kindness guiding you to be kind to people even in situations where you do not think they deserve your kindness.

Do you feel your body receive the spirit of kindness? Breathe steadily and deeply. Do you feel its warmth? Embrace the coldness or negativity and meanness exiting your body. Do not let it come back.

You are cloaked in kindness, ready for all the great doors being kind will open for you -seen and unseen. Even if you do not gain any material gain from your kindness, know that Reiki is pleased.

Your path rewards your kindness as you reward others with your kind words and thoughts.

Breathe in a big gulp of kindness one more and let go of anything standing in the way of you being kind. Open your eyes gently. Blink.

Stand and start your day.

7

Test Anxiety
Mindfulness Meditation

"There is something wonderfully bold and liberating about saying yes to our entire imperfect and messy life." –
Tara Brach

1. The sense of the unknown is one of the main triggers of test anxiety. The ability to be comfortable with our imperfect lives is an important aspect of managing your test anxiety. How can you celebrate the unknown today?

2. When you are prepared for tests, whether they are medical or a written exam, there is only so much you can do. After you prepare, you have to embrace the unknown. Preparation ensures that you have done all that

you can to put yourself in the best spot. How are you preparing for your test?

3. Whether you get favorable or unfavorable results, what can you say that you have learned from the process of preparing for your test?

4. How can you prepare for your test in three practical ways?

<u>Mindfulness Meditation For Test Anxiety #1</u>

There are a lot of thoughts running around your mind right now. Your mind is racing, but grab that last thought and let it disappear.

Let all of your thoughts simmer until they have vanished like a mist in the wind. Take note of the lightness of your eyelids caressing your eye. Take a breath as big as you can and let it out. Still your thoughts.

With each breath that you exhale, let worry fly out of your brain. Replace worry with assurance. The worries you have are blocking you. With each breath, imagine your worries weighing less and less. Your worries are lighter and lighter.

When you breath in, imagine a feeling of completion and gratitude. All of your problems have been taken care of.

Take full deep breaths and rest assured that with every breath, your worries have dissipated into thin air. They have vanished. See your strong self being guided by Reiki, covering all of your steps.

Feel the life force travel through every toe, sliding up your ankle, swimming around in your tummy, jumping up to your chest, down your arms around your fingertips, back up to your neck, throughout your face and finally to your head.

Feel it tickle your eyes, encouraging your, empowering you to see the great, worry-free life that you already have. Today let your worries rest. They will take care of themselves.

Open your eyes and make your day a great one.

<u>Mindfulness Meditation For Test Anxiety #2</u>

Smoothly shift your body to your most comfortable position. If you are already in your most comfortable position, you can stay there.

Breathe in. Breathe out. Breathe in. Breathe out. Focus on your breaths when you breath in. Breath in. Hold it for three seconds. Breathe out. Breathe in from your nose. Gather the breath from the soles of your feet and bring the breath out through your mouth.

With every deep breath, focus on the hard work that Reiki has allowed you to do. Focus on the benefits of being able to work with your mind or hands to provide for yourself and your family. Be thankful.

Exhale every single excuse that stands in the way of you not being able to do a good job on your work. Get rid of every mental block that prevents you from showing gratitude for the work that you are able to do right now.

If you are looking for a different passion or a different calling or want to continue to excel with what you are currently doing, inhale the life force. Feel it guiding you to the path that you need to take.

Exhale the particles of negativity, slothfulness, procrastination, ungratefulness, and laziness.

Inhale the joy of met guidelines and great jobs of completing your tasks to prepare you for what's to come. Do not squander the moment to work today for a better tomorrow.

Breathe out. For one more time, breathe in the joy of a job well done. Sure accolades are great, but feel the joy and pride of knowing that you did the best job that you could do. Feel grateful that you are being rewarded for the hard work that you do by Reiki.

Blink three times. Open your eyes and be productive and grateful for today.

8

OCD Mindfulness Meditation

"A mind set in its ways is wasted." –
Eric Schmidt

1. If you had to let go of all control today, how would you react? How would you want to react? What are you doing to work on the behavior you would like?
2. How are you currently coping with your OCD? Why do you want to change?
3. Who can you get to help you with your OCD today. What do you want them to remind you of if they see you engaging in this behavior?
4. What is one way you will work on overcoming your OCD today?

<u>Mindfulness Meditation For OCD #1</u>

When you are comfortable in your special place, slide into stillness. Slide into utter stillness and utmost quiet.

Do you feel your breath?

Each breath you breathe tickles your insides, calming your worry. Your worries are no longer insurmountable, they are just gentle obstacles that you can scoot by. Continue to take deep, long breaths, and feel the life force swirling within you. You can breathe out any problems that you think are too big for you to handle until they are now manageable bit by bit.

Today your goal is to focus on everything as it is. Do not try to change anything, just accept today for today. With every breath, focus on what you can do, not what you cannot do. You can be kind and gracious in every relationship that you have. You can speak life-affirming words to those around you. You can use the power of your tongue to uplift and change your situation.

If you think positive, your body and actions will follow.

Inhale a gigantic breath. Let your body take in all the positivity that deep breathing brings.

Breath it out. Rid yourself of all your worries.

One more time.

Inhale a humongous breath. Think of the great things that are going to happen today and breath it out the negative thoughts.

Now open your eyes and smile.

<u>Mindfulness Meditation For OCD #2</u>

You are in your special place. This is a place just for you. You are safe to let go of any doubts or negative thoughts you are having. Let them go somewhere else. You are too full of positivity to make room for any negativity. There is no space within you to entertain something that is not uplifting you.

Close your eyes. Inhale deeply and feel your breath go as deep into your chest as possible. Let Reiki fill your chest. Think of the abundance you will have today. Think of the extra that you will be able to share with other.

Exhale all of the distractions that are standing in the way of your abundance. They are no longer a factor. As a matter of fact, they are like a whiff of condensation. You can no longer see them. You no longer hear them. You no longer feel them.

Inhale the abundant joy that you will experience. Today is the first day of many abundantly joyful days to come. Think of everything that makes you happy. Children's laughter. The smile of a loved one. The bark of your dog. The purr of your cat. The smell of a freshly printed book.

Breathe out all of the sad things and bad news that you have heard recently. Maybe someone hurt you. That's ok. Your abundant joy is more than enough to overcome their hurt and yours. Be grateful for Reiki and the ability to overlook negativity.

Breathe in all of the abundant prosperity that you are going to have. Feel Reiki racing to your fingertips, the tips of your toes, your tongue, your brain. You are what you need to be at this very moment. Revel in it.

Breathe out any doubts about where you are supposed to be right now. Quite the noise. Inhale abundance as deeply and possible.

Open your eyes and have a great day. A day full of everything that you heart desires and a day that is in line with the universe.

9

Trauma Recovery Mindfulness Meditation

"Between stimulus and response, there's a space, in that space lies our power to choose our response, in our response lies our growth and our freedom."
Viktor Frankl

1. In what ways has trauma affected your life? Are there any positives you can glean from the situation?
2. How are you currently coping with your trauma? What is the one thing you could deal to cope with your trauma right now? What are you doing about the response you are choosing to deal with your trauma?
3. What three short-term strategies are you using to deal with your trauma? What three long-term strategies are you using to deal with your trauma?

4. How can your support group help you deal with your trauma better? How will you express that to them?

Mindfulness Meditation for Trauma Recovery #1

This mindfulness meditation is to help you cope with the pain and suffering. Be sure that you are in a comfortable place before we begin. That comfortable place could be sitting in a dignified position in a chair or lying down.

Have a pen and paper handy in case you need to write down anything later. Place your head in a comfortable position, and make sure your body is relaxed. Raise your shoulders up and hold them up before 5 seconds. Then let your shoulders release go and release all the tension out your body. You can also play soft, calming music in the background if you'd like. Take three deep breaths breathing from the very depths of your diaphragm and breathing out through your nose.

Breathe in. Breathe out. Still your thoughts. You are in a judgment-free zone.

Inhale for three counts: 1, 2, 3. And exhale for three counts: 1, 2, 3.

Inhale one more time. Exhale one more time.

Once you feel comfortable, if you feel the painful thoughts come back, that's okay. Do not try to fix the pain. Do not try to deal with the pain. Just feel it.

Breathe in deeply. If you want to cry, feel free to cry. If it feels like you will never ever get over this pain, breath, and brace that feeling filled up with all your pain. You will get over it.

Now take a breath and let the air fully out. Breathe in deeply again. Look at your thoughts neutrally. Now try to look at yourself like you're from the outside looking in. If you could describe yourself, what would it be? What's one good thing that you see about yourself? What's one area of opportunity? What can you learn from this situation?

Where do you feel the most pain? Is it in the middle of your chest or is it in the pit of your stomach? Wherever it is, zone in on your pain. Now that you've located that pain, take in a big breath and feel that the oxygen is healing the pain.

Feel grounded at this moment and know that things are going to be better. Grief and pain do not last always. The more you breathe in, the more you grow. The more you breathe in, the less grief you have. Ride the wave of breath into calmness. You are one in spirit and in mind. They are guiding you and sending rays of warmth, love and positive energy to you so that you know that you are not alone.

Feel the relaxation coming over you. Do not run away from the emotion. Now instead of feeling like the sadness, focus on the good times. The fun, the laughter, the realness. Take more deep breaths and bring energy into your body. Know that you're never alone. Replenish your broken heart with breaths and with positive affirmations.

Breathe in and then breathe out. Repeat after me, "I am loved." You are loved by yourself, and you are loved by your loved ones. The pain you are feeling shows that someone loved you and you loved someone too.

Breathe in and then breathe out. Repeat after me. "I had precious valuable time with my loved one, and I know that I will get through this." The old cliché is true: 'Time heals all wounds.'

Breathe in and then breathe out. Repeat after me. "I know

that grief and pain will not last forever." Just like anxiety, just like pain from hitting your big toe on the side of the bed, pain is temporary and one day you will not even feel the pain.

Breathe in and then breathe out. Repeat after me: "I am wiser, stronger, and I am ready for whatever lies ahead." You are strong, brave, kind and tough. You will get through this.

Breathe in and then breathe out. Hold the in between space between your next breath. Now breathe in and breath out one more time.

On three, gently open your eyes and awaken. Keep the feelings of love, calmness, and feelings of happiness with you throughout the day.

<u>Mindfulness Meditation For Trauma Recovery #2</u>

In this meditation, we're going to focus on dealing with recovering from trauma. Depression can sometimes feel like wearing sopping wet clothes. You want to dry them because you're wearing them, but it is the only pair you have. So you have to wear them wet, which can take a while. If you had a dryer you would put the clothes in there, but you do not, alas you have to let the clothes air-dry. This meditation will help the clothes dry smoother. I want to commend you for taking action for taking the first step of deciding to meditate.

For this meditation, start by being comfortable. You can be in a nice warm place where you won't be disturbed. We will need time for peace and quiet. We're going to start off breathing deeply with our diaphragm and releasing those breaths from our mouth. As we're breathing, switch out the cloud of doom and gloom above you to a cloud of white positive energy right above us. That energy is right over us. Wherever you go, you are able to get energy and positivity from it that can help make you stronger throughout the day. Every time you breathe in, that energy source gets stronger. Every time you breathe out, negativity, fear, anxiety your worries, and your depression gets weaker. The more you breathe, the stronger, your energy source will be.

Now let's imagine that we are at a beautiful lake house. You are in the middle of the forest with beautiful trees around and it smells like pine. The tall trees reach the sky and are tall and shady. You hang under the trees, and it is only you and your cloud of energy. Feel the beautiful, gentle breeze that goes across the lake while you're sending. Breath in and feel the power level raise up. Feel calm feel at peace.

Now you want to dip your feet into the lake. Do so. You are floating in the middle of the water on a raft. Float on your back and make a ripple in the water with your finger. While you float on your back, you feel that cloud in the warm sunshine giving you energy. You have no room for the depression. It is going smaller. The more you laugh and giggle and enjoy yourself in the water the more it goes away.

While you were at your favorite place on the lake, think of some of your favorite sounds besides the water. What about the laugh of your baby? The giggle of a sibling or relative? The beautiful sound of fresh water dripping on the pine needles. The more you think of beautiful images as you breathe in, the more that cloud gets powered, your depression weakens and the clothes dry. Breathe in and breathe out. With every breath, feel how much dryer your clothes are beginning to feel.

At this time, just enjoy being in this moment. Feel how your body is beginning to relax. You feel so good, warm and relaxed. You could just go to sleep on the water, but you're not going to. Now you're going to stand upon your raft. Feel the sun on you trying out your body, but feel how reinvigorated you are.

Now as you bring yourself back to your body in your critical brain, you're going to breathe in that feeling of peaceful calm and serenity. Carry the feeling with you throughout the day. And then exhale. When you do so, exhale out any negativity thoughts and feelings you may have.

Whenever you feel like your body is just soaking wet in soggy clothes, think about this wonderful energy source or your beautiful day at the beach and your lovely energy cloud that can dry you right out. You are able to feel the calmness from your breathing.

With every breath you take, imagine your white, warm ball of energy that is floating above you, replacing your tears with laughs. Imagine that warm cloud of energy replacing every negative thought you have with a positive one. Imagine that warm ball of energy arming you with calmness, strength, and positivity to right any depressive bout you may face.

Imagine a future where depression is no longer an issue for you. What does that day look like where you say goodbye to depression? What will you be wearing? What type of perfume or cologne will you wear? What will be your celebratory dinner? Are you going to celebrate with friends or by yourself.

Breathe in and then breathe out again. Call your awareness to this very moment. Enjoy the quiet calm joy that your breathing brings.

How will your hair look on the day that you beat depression? Are you going to treat yourself to all your favorite things like a massage, shopping spree, or manicure and pedicure? Keep this visualization close. Know that you are capable of using your breath to control your depression.

Breath in deeply for a 5 count this time: 1, 2, 3, 4, 5. Breathe out and let your breathe go out deeply: 1, 2, 3, 4, 5.

On the count of three, we will bring the meditation to a close. If you need to continue to meditate, feel free to do so. We are in no rush to get you to the next activity. Being mindful is all about taking your time to be present and aware at the moment on your own terms. You can go at your own pace. Whenever you are ready gently open your eyes. One. Two. Three.

Conclusion

Thank for making it through to the end of *Mindfulness Workbook For Anxiety: A Guide To Stress Relief and Anxiety Reduction With The Help of Daily Meditation*, let's hope it was informative and able to provide you with all of the tools you need to achieve your goals whatever they may be.

If you can only take one thing away from this book, please take this, please know that mindfulness can transform your life. If can be the difference between a regular life or a life that's appreciated and full of gratitude. If you are on the track to being more mindful in your everyday life, know that you are on a journey that will unleash wonderful surprises in your life.

The next step is to find a special place so you can begin your mindful meditation practice. You can even go ahead and create your list of affirmations that you can use throughout your sessions. You can revisit any of your special phrases in the book that you marked to check out at any other time. Feel free to join any support group that can help answer any questions you may have along the way. There are great resources to check out online. You can also check out location meditation groups on Craigslist or find a Meetup site. Also, try to eat healthily and sleep well. The better you take care of your body, the better your meditation session will be. Overall health also helps you to be more mindful in your day-to-day life.

Remember, that you do not have to do everything right the right time when you meditate. As you progress in your practice, you will continue to improve. Embrace the journey. Lastly, do not stop learning.

Mindfulness Workbook For Anxiety: A Guide To Stress Relief and Anxiety Reduction With The Help of Daily Meditation is a great foundation to have, but continue to build on it. Continue to learn more about how the benefits of mindfulness meditation affect you. You can also continue to work on mindfulness by using guided meditations until you are at the point where you can do the meditations on your own without the help of guided steps. This journey is to last a lifetime and the more prepared you are the more you will be prepared to sustain and improve your mindfulness meditation practice along the way.

Finally, if you found this book useful in any way, a review on Amazon is always appreciated!

Additional Resources

The resources in this chapter will help you expand your mindfulness meditation practice to help you cope with your anxiety.

Apps

- Aura
- Insight Timer

Websites

- The Omega Institute YouTube Channel
- PalouseMindfulness.com
- Anxiety Disorders Association of America

Books

- *Calming Your Anxious Mind: How Mindfulness and Compassion Can Free You from Anxiety, Fear, and Panic, Second Edition.* Jeffrey Brantley
- *The Mindful Way Through Anxiety: Break Free from Chronic Worry and Reclaim your Life.* Lizabeth Roemer and Susan Orsillo
- *The Generalized Anxiety Disorder Workbook: A Comprehensive CBT Guide for Coping with Uncertainty, Worry, and Fear.* Michel Dugas and Melissa Robichaud
- *Face Your Fears: A Proven Plan to Beat Anxiety, Panic, Phobias, and Obsessions.* David Tolin

<u>Calming Sounds</u>

- Rain sounds
- Ocean waves
- Birds chirping
- Lullaby music
- Crickets
- White noise

My Other Books

Anxiety Relief for Kids

Have you noticed that your child is constantly tense all the time? Are they displaying irrational fears occasionally? Moments where they seem to be crippled by fear that it disrupts their daily function? What you could be dealing with is a child with anxiety.

Everyone worries. That is a part of our normal range of human emotion. Even children have worries of their own. But it is when those worries cross over from regular worrying to excessive worrying that starts to disrupt your daily routine that it becomes a problem. Believe it or not, anxiety doesn't just affect adults, but children can be victims of this condition too. **Anxiety is one of the most prevalent disorders in America today**, and it can be challenging for both children and adults who are dealing with this condition. It can also be equally as challenging for the parents, because what can you do to help make it better for your child? How do you protect them from feeling this way?

Anxiety Relief for Kids is a complete workbook which will help your child overcome their worries, stress, anger, depression, panic attacks, and fears with ***proven strategies*** that work.

In this book, you will learn how to:

- Understand anxiety and how it is affecting your child
- Discover anxiety relief strategies and build your own activities toolbox
- How to parent an anxious child

- Engaging games and crafts that you can do to help your child work through their anxiety
- The difference between depression and anger
- What separates panic attacks from fears

The exercises, methods, and strategies which you will uncover in this book will shed light on the importance of helping your child overcome anxiety. More importantly, it is a guide for all parents with anxious children about what *you can do* to help your child through this very challenging emotion that they are dealing with. **All the strategies you have ever wanted to help your child find their happiness again is right here**. They do not have to live a life that is crippled by worries and fears. It is possible to change all that. Improve their self-esteem and help your child find their self-worth once more by freeing them from the grip of anxiety.

This book is packed with all the useful information that every parent with an anxious child needs to help make a real difference in the way that their child deals with anxiety. Overcoming anxiety is going to require practice, time, and effort, and this book will show you just what you need to do to help your child through the process. Put a stop to your child's anxiety once and for all with the *Anxiety Relief for Kids* workbook.

The Anxiety Workbook for Teens

This book will discuss how to deal with the difficulties of being a teen and a young adult in today's society. It can also be a tool for adults who want to better understand the struggles of teens or young adults in their lives. It is easy to forget how difficult it is to be a teenager and young adult, and how there are stressors in the life of today's teens that their parents or guardians did not have to deal with.

Using real-world examples and practical advice, we will discuss stress and anxiety, where it comes from, and how to deal with it. It assures teens that their feelings are normal and valid and gives them tools to deal with these feelings.

- Panic attacks: why they are normal, why it's not your fault, and how to deal with them.

- Social anxiety: what it is, do you have it, and challenges to complete to help overcome it.

Shyness is discussed, assuring the reader that it is a personality trait that is not inherently negative, although it can make life difficult.

- Practical advice is given on how to overcome your shyness.
- Practical advice is provided on how to disguise your shyness while working to overcome it.

Teens and young adults can get to know themselves better with the section on self-perception. The way you perceive yourself isn't always accurate to who you really are. This tool will aid in breaking things down and making them clear.

- Worksheets to help teens and young adults get to know themselves better, identifying strengths they want to nurture, and weaknesses they want to improve.

The myriad causes of stress in the life of today's teen and young adult are examined, with real-world examples.

- The most common causes of stress amongst teens and young adults are discussed, and practical ways to deal with these stressors are provided.
- Techniques for handling and reducing stress in general are provided, along with encouragement for the individual to develop ways that are most natural and helpful to them

Fear is analfyzed. What is fear? Where does it come from, and what is its purpose?

- Practical advice on how to manage fear and live a normal life
- How to recognize and overcome phobias

Depression is discussed at length, assuring the reader that what they are feeling is normal, and not their fault and imploring the reader to ask for help if they need it, as well as the warning signs that they should not handle their depression alone.

- Discussion on sadness versus depression
- Worksheet to identify and facilitate discussion about depression
- Practical advice on how to live with and overcome depression, and keep it from coming back

Self-confidence is important! What it is and how to get it.

- Techniques provided to aid in self-empowerment
- How to use positive affirmations in the quest for self-confidence
- The importance of setting goals, and worksheets to facilitate this

The reader is continually reminded that they are of value as they are now. Experiencing stress, anxiety, have phobias, or depression does not make them any lesser. This is a tool for self-knowledge and self-improvement.

About the author

In her teenage years, Rachel Stone has struggled with severe anxiety. During this time the practices of compassion and meditation helped her face her difficulties through her young adulthood.

She became passionate about traditional psychotherapy, has been exploring yoga and meditation and started implementing mindfulness to achieve mental and emotional healing. The practice of daily meditation had an incredible impact on her life and has helped her fully conquer anxiety and eliminating panic attacks.

In her first book "Anxiety Relief for Kids" she offers practical strategies to calm anxious minds, transform negative emotions, and facilitate greater self-acceptance, freedom and inner peace, teaching parents and children how to use the most up-to-date evidence-based strategies.

She takes readers on a journey that make use of mindfulness and other alternative techniques to finally achieve mental peace. She also specializes in CBT for children, adolescents, and adults with anxiety disorders, obsessive-compulsive disorder (OCD), and depression.

In her books, she advocates that mental health comes from an approach that looks at all aspects of the self; physical, mental, emotional and spiritual.

It is important to enjoy life and we have the inner power to transform our traumas and habitual patterns that keep us stuck in perpetual state of stress, anxiety, depression, or addiction and step into greater freedom and peace breaking the cycle of fear.

www.ingramcontent.com/pod-product-compliance
Lightning Source LLC
La Vergne TN
LVHW031326190726
843493LV00013B/3051